where did _____ go

written by: Shana King
Illustrated by: Nevaeh Peters

Copyright © 2023 by Shana King
ISBN: 979-8-218-15710-4

All rights reserved.

No portion of this book may be reproduced in any form without written permission from the publisher or author, except as permitted by U.S. copyright law.

Dedicated to the greatest loves of my life.
Greg, Nevaeh, Brian, Mattea, and Arwen

When I was young, the trouble started.
The parents I knew suddenly parted.

Why it happened, I don't know.

My father left.... where did he go?

**The weekend came and he came back!
He even took me to the dog track!**

Why he dropped me off when we were done, I don't know.

Then he left.... where did he go?

Whenever he came,
I had a lot of fun.
We played games
and I even won!

But again he dropped me off. Why? I don't know.

Then he left.... where did he go?

The next week came and we got on a plane! We even had to fly in the rain!

We went to a place that was a lot of fun.
There were a lot of rides and a lot of sun.

The week then ended and we had to go.

He left me again.... where did he go?

The next week I waited
for him to show.
But he never came....
where did he go?

Week in...

week out...

I waited and waited.

Me being alone I really hated.

Every day I would wait by the phone.

But every day, I was alone.

I watched the clock but he didn't show.
What did I do wrong?
Where did he go?

The years that went
by were really tough.

Why didn't he come?
Wasn't I
important enough?

I thought it was my fault.
Why? I don't know.

But he never came back...
where did he go?

**The years went by,
I started to grow.
Where he was, I didn't know.**

**When I was a teenager, he was found.
He had moved out of town.**

He never reached out.
Why?
I don't know.

But at least I didn't have to ask...where did he go?

When I became an adult, I had a lot of friends.
They all became family.
No matter what I did, they all stayed around me.

It took some time with
help from my friends,
to realize that him not coming
back wasn't the end.

I was loved, I was needed,
I wasn't alone.
All of my friends made
me feel at home.

I didn't know before but my friends helped me learn, being loved by other people is something you don't have to earn.

I finally learned that his problems were his.

I have to tell you the truth and the truth is this...

Sometimes it's not easy, sometimes it takes time. Some days you're upset, some days you'll feel fine.

(And that is okay!)

It's hard not to feel
like you did something bad
Like you didn't listen,
or you made them mad.

But please know it is
NOT YOUR FAULT
that they're not around.

I learned that your family
can be the people you found.

But these feelings are big
and they can be tough.

You are loved...

you are special...

YOU ARE MORE THAN ENOUGH.

Take it from me,
I've been where you are.

It took time, but with
help I've come very far.

There is one last thing
I think you should know.

Love yourself....

you'll be amazed at
how far you can go!

"Be the person you needed when you were younger."

— Ayesha Siddiqi